TABLE OF CONTENTS

"

He established a testimony in Jacob
and appointed a law in Israel,
which he commanded our fathers
to teach to their children,
that the next generation might know them,
the children yet unborn,
and arise and tell them to their children,
so that they should set their hope in God
and not forget the works of God,
but keep his commandments.

"

PSALMS 78:5-7

To
Donna,
our children,
our grandchildren,
and children yet unborn

"

Give your children big truths they can grow
into rather than light explanations they will
grow out of.

"

TEDD TRIPP

"

I learned more about Christianity from my
mother than from all the theologians in England.

"

JOHN WESLEY

INTRODUCTION

Dr. Thomas K. Ascol

Psalm 78 casts a multi-generational vision for the people of God. Asaph declares his intention to pass on to his children that which he and his generation learned from their fathers. By doing so, his children, in turn, can teach their children. "He established a testimony in Jacob and appointed a law in Israel, which he commanded our fathers to teach to their children, that the next generation might know them, the children yet unborn, and arise and tell them to their children" (Psalm 78:5-6).

The Bible teaches that children are "a heritage from the Lord" and that "the fruit of the womb is His reward" (Psalm 127:3). Each child is a gift from God. This makes parents stewards of God, entrusted with one (or more) of His greatest blessings. It also means that those who work with children are involved in a high calling.

The Truth and Grace Memory Books (*TAG* books) are designed to help parents, churches and children's workers as they fulfill that calling. Three primary ingredients are found in each book.

9

First and foremost is the Word of God. Several passages have been carefully selected for memorization. All Scripture throughout the Scripture Memory section is in the English Standard Version. Key Bible verses as well as longer portions are designed to introduce children to the overall scope and purpose of God's creative, providential and redemptive activity. The student who completes all three books will memorize (among other texts) the Ten Commandments, the Beatitudes, the Lord's prayer, 1 Corinthians 13, various Psalms (including 119!), plus all the books of the Bible.

Why place such an emphasis on memorizing Scripture? Listen to the Psalmist's answer: "I have stored up your word in my heart that I might not sin against You" (Psalm 119:11). Furthermore, consider the great promise God makes in Isaiah 55:10–11: "For as the rain and the snow come down from heaven, and do not return there but water the earth, making it bring forth and sprout, giving seed to the sower and bread to the eater, so shall my word be that goes out from my mouth; it shall not return to me empty, but it shall accomplish that which I purpose, and shall succeed in the thing for which I sent it." God's Spirit uses the Scripture to speak to adults and children of all ages, calling them to faith in Christ and directing in the paths of real discipleship. Therefore, as a parent who prays for the salvation and spiritual growth of your child, you must be diligent in teaching him or her the Word of God.

A second element in the workbook is a selection of sound Christian hymns to be learned and memorized. Many of these are familiar (such as the Doxology) and can be learned by very small children. Others are not so well-known but are profound in their communication of biblical truth. In all, more than 2 dozen great hymns of the faith are included.

A WORD ABOUT CATECHISMS

The third, and perhaps least familiar, ingredient are catechisms. A good catechism is a very effective tool in the hands of a dedicated parent or teacher. Each *TAG* book is built around a trustworthy, Baptist catechism. That term —"Baptist catechism"—may sound strange to many modern Baptists. They may think, as I did early in my life, that "catechism" is a Roman Catholic, Lutheran or, at best, Presbyterian word.

Of course, that simply is not true. "Catechize" is anglicized version of the Greek word, *katekeo,* which simply means "to teach." It appears, in various forms, several times in the Greek New Testament (it is translated as "taught" in Luke 1:4 and Acts 18:25).

Anyone, then, who has been taught has in some sense been catechized. But the word came to refer to a specific type of instruction early in church history. New Christians were taught the essentials of the faith by learning how to answer specific questions, which were eventually grouped together and came to be referred to simply as a "catechism."

Tom Nettles has called the 16th-century Protestant Reformation the "golden age" of catechisms. In 1562 what is arguably the most influential one of all was published as the Heidelberg Catechism. Leading reformers, most notably Martin Luther and John Calvin, produced catechisms to teach both the essentials and distinctives of their faith. In the next century, the first modern Baptists followed suit.

Early Baptist leaders regarded catechetical instruction as a valuable method to teach both children and adults the doctrinal content of the Bible. Keach's Catechism (whose author, Benjamin Keach—a 17th-century English Baptist— modeled it after the Shorter Catechism of the Westminster Assembly) was widely used among Baptists in both England and America. Charles Spurgeon (19th-century English Baptist leader) revised it slightly and reissued it for use in the Metropolitan Tabernacle.

Early Southern Baptists freely employed catechisms. One of the first publications which the Sunday School Board produced was a catechism by James Boyce, founder and first President of Southern Seminary. John Broadus also wrote a catechism which was published by the board in the 19th century. Lottie Moon used a catechism in her missionary work in China.

The *TAG* Books stand firmly in this stream of Orthodox, Protestant and Baptist catechetical instruction. Each of the three books is based on a specific catechism. *The Baptist Catechism* is reproduced in the second book, and we use this original version of the catechism so that it matches *The Baptist Catechism* set to music (which can be purchased from Founders Ministries). A simpler, more elementary one, *A Catechism for Boys and Girls*, is used in the first and *The Heidelberg Catechism for Baptists* (which draws on *The Orthodox Catechism* of 1680) is used in the third.

A WORD TO PARENTS

Raising children in the 21st century is challenging, to say the least. The temptation on parents to merely get by is great. Sometimes moms and dads simply want to make it through with the fewest possible conflicts. When this attitude is adopted parents become passive and children learn to be manipulative and the result is that neither parents nor children are happy. Though tragic, it is sadly not uncommon to see Christian homes where parents have defaulted on the responsibilities that God has entrusted to them.

Teaching their children the Word of God is at the forefront of responsibilities for Christian parents. God specifically calls Christian parents to raise their children "in the discipline and instruction of the Lord" (Ephesians 6:4). You cannot be passive and fulfill this responsibility to "bring them up" in the proper way. Prayer, discipline, godly example, and consistent, continuous, clear instruction are required.

The comprehensive nature of this responsibility is spelled out in Deuteronomy 6:4–6.

> "Hear, O Israel: The LORD our God, the LORD is one. You shall love the LORD your God with all your heart and with all your soul and with all your might. And these words that I command you today shall be on your heart. You shall teach them diligently to your children, and shall talk of them when you sit in your house, and when you walk by the way, and when you lie down, and when you rise."

In the face of such a daunting responsibility I cannot overstate the value of a well-constructed catechism to help parents in this work. By learning such a catechism a child (or adult for that matter) will be introduced to the overall biblical scheme of salvation. Such discipline will frame the mind for receiving and understanding every part of the Bible. A good catechism trains a person to read the Bible theologically.

God places the responsibility for raising children squarely on the shoulders of their parents. It is not primarily the job of church leaders or the pastor. If you are a parent then recognizing and accepting this responsibility is one of the most important things you can do. If you do not invest your time and effort to teach your children about God, be assured someone else will. Your children will be discipled by someone. They may get their ideas about God primarily from television, music or social media. If so, then they are likely to be taught that God, if He exists at all, is an irrelevant, indulgent being that is little more than a nice, kindly old man. If you do not teach your children truth and righteousness, be assured that there are a multitude of teachers in this world who would deceive them into thinking that truth is personal and morality is relative.

As a pastor I have spent my life teaching the church I serve to believe sound doctrine and to stand against the false teachers of our age whose views would destroy the souls of our young people. As a Christian you have every right to expect that the sermons and teaching heard in your church will reinforce the godly principles which you are trying to teach at home. But you have no right to expect your church to take the place of the home. God has given to parents the responsibility of teaching their children divine truth.

The *TAG* books have been designed to help you fulfill that assignment. The emphasis is on memorization. Some modern educators question the wisdom of teaching young children to memorize. Concern usually centers on the fear that the child is merely committing to memory meaningless words. This is a real danger—that we will be satisfied with hearing our children merely recite back to us words and sentences of which they have no understanding. That is why parents should carefully teach their children the material in these books. Personal understanding should always be the goal of our teaching. But understanding grows over time (mine has; hasn't yours?). Truth committed to memory provides the building blocks for such growth.

I originally produced the *TAG* books in the late 1990s for the parents and children in Grace Baptist Church of Cape Coral, Florida. I borrowed from and leaned on the work of many people, including Paul Settle, Fred Malone, Bill Ascol, Karen Leach, Judy Veilleux and, of course, my wife, Donna. Founders Press first published the *TAG* books in 2000 and then again in 2005. For this new edition I owe a debt of gratitude to Jared and Heather Longshore, whose determination, thoughtfulness and creativity have made this work more accessible to a new generation of parents and children. It is a testimony to God's grace in reviving the work of His gospel that they continue to find a wide readership. My prayer has been and remains that the Lord will use these books to help parents raise generations of men and women who are mighty in His Word and Spirit and who will take the wonderful news of Jesus Christ to the remaining hard places in our world.

Donna and I loved catechizing our children. Now we love watching our children who have become parents catechizing our grandchildren. It is to those children, their spouses and our grandchildren that the Truth and Grace Memory Books are dedicated.

HOW TO USE THIS MEMORY BOOK

I remember how intimidated I was when Donna and I made our first attempts to start catechizing our firstborn. After many starts and stops and lots of mistakes, we finally settled into a healthy rhythm of incorporating questions from the catechism both in set times and informal times with her and her siblings. Following are some of the lessons we learned along the way.

Discuss the material being memorized with your child. This should be done during the actual memorization as well as at other opportune times in the day. Daily experiences and observations provide a world of opportunities to illustrate and apply God's Word. For example, those pesky night frights that young children occasionally have become wonderful occasions to comfortingly remind them that, though we cannot see God, He always sees us.

Take time to define difficult terms. Question your child in order to discover the level of his understanding. When you feel that understanding is being achieved, pray with and for the child, including in your prayer some of the concepts just discussed. Expect your children to learn, and rejoice with them over their growth in knowledge and understanding of God's Word.

No matter what the age of your children, if you will begin immediately, and continue consistently, to teach them with this workbook, you will instill in them a comprehensive awareness of the Bible's whole system of revealed truth. Obviously, the earlier a child begins, the better. But these books have been designed to be useful to young people as well to children and preschoolers.

Following are some specific suggestions that come from my experience.

1. Make this workbook something very special in your child's life. Emphasize the importance of learning God's Word. If you are genuinely excited about it, most likely your children will be also.

2. Incorporate it into your regular time of family prayer and devotion. After you have read a portion of God's Word, or some Bible story book, and have prayed, take a few minutes to work on a specific verse or question. Learn to sing the hymns together as a family. You can do it! You simply have to make the effort.

3. Encourage precise memorization. If they are going to spend the time and effort to learn it, they might as well learn it accurately.

4. Be very positive. Try not to let the workbook become a battleground where a contest of the wills (child's vs. parent's) occurs. This does not mean that you let the child dictate when he will or will not work on the material. Rather, do not let yourself get into the position where you are violating biblical principles (by employing

rage, sarcasm, ridicule, empty threats, etc.) in your zeal to have your child learn the Bible! Instead, make it an enjoyable—and at times, even fun—time. Donna and I would often let our children ask us the questions.

5. Date and sign each step. At the back of the workbook there are places for the parent to signify that the student has completed the assignments. Treat each one as a significant milestone and encourage your child to keep progressing.

6. Go at your child's own rate. Children, like adults, learn differently and at different tempos. The workbook is designed so that the material can be covered as quickly or slowly as needed. Do not hesitate to move beyond the stated age levels. Remember, these are merely suggestions.

7. Discuss the content of the verses, catechism questions or hymns being learned. Help your child understand what they are saying. Remember, the goal is spiritual understanding, not mechanical regurgitation.

8. Review. Avoid placing such an emphasis on advancement that your child is tempted to utilize only his or her short-term rather than long-term memory.

9. Rejoice. Your child is learning Bible truths which some adults will never know. Thank the Lord for the privilege of teaching your children about Him. Be encouraged as you hear them reciting the Word of God and expressing important biblical truths.

10. Pray. Ask God to drive His Word deep into the heart and conscience of each child. Pray that He will send His Spirit to teach them inwardly the truth about sin and judgment, heaven and hell, Jesus and salvation. As you diligently teach your children, labor in prayer for them until you see Christ being formed in them.

11. Encourage other parents. We all need it. Make a conscious effort to give it. Training our children in the way of the Lord is a high calling. We are constantly tempted to neglect it. We all fail at some point and at some time. Resolve to be an encourager.

"

Believe me... the church of God will never be preserved without catechesis.

"

JOHN CALVIN

THE BAPTIST CATECHISM

1. Who is the first and chiefest being?
   God is the first and chiefest being (Isaiah
   44:6; 48:12; Psalm 97:9).

2. Ought everyone to believe there is a God?
   Everyone ought to believe there is a God
   (Hebrews 11:6); and it is their great sin and
   folly who do not (Psalm 14:1).

3. How may we know there is a God?
   The light of nature in man and the works of
   God plainly declare there is a God (Romans
   1:19, 20; Psalm 19:1, 2, 3; Acts 17:24); but His
   Word and Spirit only do it fully and
   effectually for the salvation of sinners (1
   Corinthians 2:10; 2 Timothy 3:15, 16).

4.   What is the Word of God?
      The Holy Scriptures of the Old and New
      Testament are the Word of God, and the
      only certain rule of faith and obedience (2
      Timothy 3:16; Ephesians 2:20).

5.   May all men make use of the Holy Scriptures?
      All men are not only permitted, but
      commanded and exhorted to read, hear, and
      understand the Holy Scriptures (John 5:38;
      John 17:17–19; Revelation 1:3; Acts 8:30).

6.   What things are chiefly contained in the
      Holy Scriptures?
      The Holy Scriptures chiefly contain what
      man ought to believe concerning God, and
      what duty God requireth of man (2 Timothy
      1:13; 3:15, 16).

7.   What is God?
      God is a Spirit (John 4:24), infinite (Job 11:7,
      8, 9), eternal (Psalm 110:2), and
      unchangeable (James 1:17) in His being
      (Exodus 3:14), wisdom (Psalm 147:5), power
      (Revelation 4:8), holiness (Revelation 15:4),
      justice, goodness, and truth (Exodus 34:6).

8.   Are there more gods than one?
      There is but one only, the living and true
      God (Deuteronomy 6:4; Jeremiah 10:10).

9. How many persons are there in the Godhead?
There are three persons in the godhead, the Father, the Son, and the Holy Spirit; and these three are one God, the same in essence, equal in power and glory (1 John 5:7; Matthew 28:19).

10. What are the decrees of God?
The decrees of God are His eternal purpose according to the counsel of His will, whereby, for His own glory, He hath foreordained whatsoever comes to pass (Ephesians 1:4, 11; Romans 9:22–23; Isaiah 46:10; Lamentations 3:37).

11. How doth God execute His decrees?
God executeth His decrees in the works of creation and providence.

12. What is the work of creation?
The work of creation is God's making all things of nothing, by the word of His power, in the space of six days, and all very good (Genesis 1 throughout; Hebrews 11:3).

13. How did God create man?
God created man, male and female, after His own image, in knowledge, righteousness, and holiness, with dominion over the creatures (Genesis 1:26, 27, 28; Colossians 3:10, Ephesians 4:24).

14. What are God's works of providence?
God's works of providence are His most holy (Psalm 145:17), wise (Isaiah 28:29, Psalm 104:24), and powerful preserving (Hebrews 1:3) and governing all His creatures, and all their actions (Psalm 103:19; Matthew 10:29, 30, 31).

15. What special act of providence did God exercise towards man in the estate wherein He was created?
When God had created man, He entered into a covenant of life with him upon condition of perfect obedience: forbidding him to eat of the tree of the knowledge of good and evil, upon pain of death (Galatians 3:12; Genesis 2:17).

16. Did our first parents continue in the estate wherein they were created?
Our first parents being left to the freedom of their own will, fell from the estate wherein they were created, by sinning against God (Genesis 3:6, 7, 8, 13; Ecclesiastes 7:29).

17. What is sin?
Sin is any want of conformity unto, or transgression of, the law of God (1 John 3:4).

18. What was the sin whereby our first parents fell from the estate wherein they were created?
The sin whereby our first parents fell from the estate wherein they were created, was their eating the forbidden fruit (Genesis 3:6, 12, 16, 17).

19. Did all mankind fall in Adam's first transgression?
The covenant being made with Adam, not only for himself but for his posterity, all mankind descending from him by ordinary generation sinned in him, and fell with him in his first transgression (Genesis 2:16, 17; Romans 5:12; 1 Corinthians 15:21, 22).

20. Into what estate did the fall bring mankind?
The fall brought mankind into an estate of sin and misery (Romans 5:12).

21. Wherein consists the sinfulness of that estate whereinto man fell?
The sinfulness of that estate whereinto man fell, consists in the guilt of Adam's first sin, the want of original righteousness, and the corruption of his whole nature, which is commonly called original sin; together with all actual transgressions which proceed from it (Romans 5:12, to the end; Ephesians 2:1, 2, 3; James 1:14, 15; Matthew 15:19).

22. What is the misery of that estate whereinto man fell?
All mankind by their fall lost communion with God (Genesis 3:8, 10, 24), are under His wrath and curse (Ephesians 2:2, 3; Galatians 3:10), and so made liable to all miseries in this life, to death itself, and to the pains of hell for ever (Lamentations 3:39; Romans 6:23; Matthew 25:41, 46).

23. Did God leave all mankind to perish in the estate of sin and misery?
God having out of His mere good pleasure, from all eternity, elected some to everlasting life (Ephesians 1:4, 5), did enter into a covenant of grace, to deliver them out of the estate of sin and misery, and to bring them into an estate of salvation by a Redeemer (Romans 3:20–22; Galatians 3:21, 22).

24. Who is the Redeemer of God's elect?
The only Redeemer of God's elect is the Lord Jesus Christ (1 Timothy 2:5, 6); who, being the eternal Son of God, became man (John 1:14; Galatians 4:4), and so was and continueth to be God and man in two distinct natures, and one person for ever (Romans 9:5; Luke 1:35; Colossians 2:9; Hebrews 7:24, 25).

25. How did Christ, being the Son of God become man?
Christ the Son of God became man by taking to Himself a true body (Hebrews 2:14, 17; 10:5), and a reasonable soul (Matthew 26:38); being conceived by the power of the Holy Spirit in the womb of the Virgin Mary, and born of her (Luke 1:27, 31, 34, 35, 42; Galatians 4:4), yet without sin (Hebrews 4:15; 7:26).

26. What offices doth Christ execute as our Redeemer?
Christ as our Redeemer executeth the offices of a prophet, of a priest, and of king, both in His estate of humiliation and exaltation (Acts 3:22; Hebrews 12:25; 2 Corinthians 13:3; Hebrews 5:5, 6, 7; 7:25; Psalm 2:6; Isaiah 9:6, 7; Matthew 21:5; Psalm 2:8–11).

27. How doth Christ execute the office of a prophet?
Christ executeth the office of prophet in revealing to us, by His Word and Spirit, the will of God for our salvation (John 1:18; 1 Peter 1:10,11, 12; John 15:15; and 20:31).

28. How doth Christ execute the office of a priest?
Christ executeth the office of priest in His once offering up Himself a sacrifice to satisfy divine justice (Hebrews 9:14, 28) and reconcile us to God (Hebrews 2:17), and in making continual intercession for us (Hebrews 7:24, 25).

29. How doth Christ execute the office of king?
Christ executeth the office of a king, in subduing us to Himself (Acts 15:14, 15, 16), in ruling (Isaiah 33:22), and defending us (Isaiah 32:1, 2), and in restraining and conquering all His and our enemies (1 Corinthians 15:25; Psalm 110 throughout).

30. Wherein did Christ's humiliation consist?
Christ's humiliation consisted in His being born, and that in a low condition (Luke 2:7), made under the law (Galatians 4:4), undergoing the miseries of this life (Hebrews 12:2, 3; Isaiah 53:2, 3), the wrath of God (Luke 22:44; Matthew 27:46), and the cursed death of the cross (Philippians 2:8); in being buried (1 Corinthians 15:3,4), and continuing under the power of death for a time (Acts 2:24, 25, 26, 27, 31; Matthew 12:40).

31. Wherein consisteth Christ's exaltation?
Christ's exaltation consisteth in His rising again from the dead on the third day (1 Corinthians 15:4), in ascending up into heaven (Mark 16:19), in sitting at the right hand of God the Father (Ephesians 1:20), and in coming to judge the world at the last day (Acts 1: 11; 17:31).

32. How are we made partakers of the redemption purchased by Christ?
We are made partakers of the redemption purchased by Christ, by the effectual application of it to us (John 1:11,12) by His Holy Spirit (Titus 3:5,6).

33. How doth the Spirit apply to us the redemption purchased by Christ?
The Spirit applieth to us the redemption purchased by Christ, by working faith in us (Ephesians 1:13, 14; John 6:37, 39; Ephesians 2:8), and thereby uniting us to Christ, in our effectual calling (Ephesians 3:17; 1 Corinthians 1:9).

34. What is effectual calling?

Effectual calling is the work of God's Spirit (2 Timothy 1:9; 2 Thessalonians 2:13, 14), whereby convincing us of our sin and misery (Acts 2:37), enlightening our minds in the knowledge of Christ (Acts 26:18), and renewing our wills (Ezekiel 36:26, 27), He doth persuade and enable us to embrace Jesus Christ freely offered to us in the gospel (John 6:44, 45; Philippians 2:13).

35. What benefits do they that are effectually called partake of in this life?

They that are effectually called do in this life partake of justification (Romans 8:30), adoption (Ephesians 1:5), sanctification, and the several benefits which in this life do either accompany or flow from them (1 Corinthians 1:30).

36. What is justification?

Justification is an act of God's free grace, wherein He pardoneth all our sins (Romans 3:24, 25; and 4:6, 7, 8), and accepteth us as righteous in His sight (2 Corinthians 5:19, 21), only for the righteousness of Christ imputed to us (Romans 5:17–19), and received by faith alone (Galatians 2:16; Philippians 3:9).

37. What is adoption?
Adoption is an act of God's free grace (1 John 3:1), whereby we are received into the number and have a right to all the privileges of the sons of God (John 1:12; Romans 8:14–17).

38. What is sanctification?
Sanctification is the work of God's free grace (2 Thessalonians 2:13), whereby we are renewed in the whole man after the image of God (Ephesians 4:23, 24), and are enabled more and more to die unto sin, and live unto righteousness (Romans 6:4, 6; 8:1).

39. What are the benefits which in this life do accompany or flow from justification, adoption, and sanctification?
The benefits which in this life do accompany or flow from justification, adoption, and sanctification, are assurance of God's love, peace of conscience (Romans 5:1, 2, 5), joy in the Holy Spirit (Romans 5:5, 17), increase of grace (Proverbs 4:18), and perseverance therein to the end (1 John 5:13; 1 Peter 1:5).

40. What benefits do believers receive from Christ at their death?

The souls of believers are at their death made perfect in holiness (Hebrews 12:23), and do immediately pass into glory (2 Corinthians 5:1, 6, 8; Philippians 1:23; Luke 23:43); and their bodies being still united to Christ (1 Thessalonians 4:14), do rest in their graves (Isaiah 57:2) till the resurrection (Job 19:26, 27).

41. What benefits do believers receive from Christ at the resurrection?

At the resurrection believers, being raised up in glory (1 Corinthians 15:43), shall be openly acknowledged, and acquitted in the day of judgment (Matthew 25:23; Matthew 10:32), and made perfectly blessed, both in soul and body, in the full enjoyment of God (1 John 3:2; 1 Corinthians 13:12) to all eternity (1 Thessalonians 4:17, 18).

42. But what shall be done to the wicked at their death?

The souls of the wicked shall, at their death, be cast into the torments of hell, and their bodies lie in their graves, till the resurrection and judgment of the great day (Luke 16:23, 24; Acts 2:24; Jude 5, 7; 1 Peter 3:19; Psalm 49:14).

43. What shall be done to the wicked, at the day of judgment?
At the day of judgment the bodies of the wicked, being raised out of their graves, shall be sentenced, together with their souls, to unspeakable torments with the devil and his angels forever (John 5:28, 29; Matthew 25:41, 46; 2 Thessalonians 1:8, 9).

44. What is the duty which God requireth of man?
The duty which God requireth of man is, obedience to His revealed will (Micah 6:8; 1 Samuel 15:22).

45. What did God at first reveal to man for the rule of his obedience?
The rule which God at first revealed to man for his obedience, was the moral law (Romans 2:14, 15, and 10:5).

46. Where is the moral law summarily comprehended?
The moral law is summarily comprehended in the Ten Commandments (Deuteronomy 10:4; Matthew 19:17).

47. What is the sum of the Ten Commandments?
The sum of the Ten Commandments is, to love the Lord our God, with all our heart, with all our soul, with all our strength, and with all our mind; and our neighbor as ourselves (Matthew 22:37–40).

48. What is the preface to the Ten Commandments?
The preface to the Ten Commandments is in these words; I am the Lord thy God which have brought thee out of the land of Egypt, out of the house of bondage (Exodus 20:2).

49. What doth the preface to the Ten Commandments teach us?
The preface to the Ten Commandments teacheth us that because God is the Lord, and our God and redeemer, therefore we are bound to keep all His commandments (Luke 1:74, 75; 1 Peter 1:15–19).

50. Which is the first commandment?
The first commandment is, Thou shalt have no other gods before Me (Exodus 20:3).

51. What is required in the first commandment?
The first commandment requireth us to know and acknowledge God to be the only true God and our God (1 Chronicles 28:9; Deuteronomy 26:17), and to worship and glorify Him accordingly (Matthew 4:10; Psalm 29:2).

52. What is forbidden in the first commandment?
The first commandment forbiddeth the
denying (Psalm 14: 1), or not worshipping
and glorifying the true God (Romans 1:21), as
God and our God (Psalm 81:10, 11), and the
giving of that worship and glory to any other,
which is due unto Him alone (Romans 1:25,
26).

53. What are we especially taught by these
words before Me, in the first commandment?
These words before Me, in the first
commandment teach us, that God, who seeth
all things, taketh notice of and is much
displeased with the sin of having any other
god (Exodus 8:5, to the end).

54. Which is the second commandment?
The second commandment is, Thou shalt not
make unto thee any graven image, or any
likeness of anything that is in heaven above,
or that is in the earth beneath, or that is in
the water under the earth; thou shalt not bow
down thyself to them, nor serve them: for I
the Lord thy God am a jealous God, visiting
the iniquity of the fathers upon the children
unto the third and fourth generation of them
that hate Me; and shewing mercy unto
thousands of them that love Me, and keep
My commandments (Exodus 20:4, 5, 6).

55. What is required in the second commandment?
The second commandment requireth the receiving, observing, and keeping pure and entire all such religious worship and ordinances, as God hath appointed in His Word (Deuteronomy 32:46; Matthew 23:20; Acts 2:42).

56. What is forbidden in the second commandment?
The second commandment forbiddeth the worshipping of God by images (Deuteronomy 4:15–19; Exodus 32:5, 8), or any other way not appointed in His Word (Deuteronomy 7:31, 32).

57. What are the reasons annexed to the second commandment?
The reasons annexed to the second commandment are, God's sovereignty over us (Psalm 45:2, 3, 6), His propriety in us (Psalm 45:11), and the zeal He hath to His own worship (Exodus 34:13, 14).

58. Which is the third commandment?
The third commandment is, Thou shalt not take the name of the Lord thy God in vain; for the Lord will not hold him guiltless that taketh His name in vain (Exodus 20:7).

59. What is required in the third commandment?
The third commandment requireth the holy
and reverent use of God's names (Matthew
6:9; Deuteronomy 28:58), titles (Psalm 68:4),
attributes (Revelation 15:3, 4), ordinances,
(Malachi 1:11, 14), word (Psalm 136:1, 2) and
works (Job 36:24).

60. What is forbidden in the third commandment?
The third commandment forbiddeth all
profaning and abusing of anything whereby
God makes Himself known (Malachi 1:6, 7,
12; 2:2; 3:14).

61. What is the reason annexed to the third
commandment?
The reason annexed to the third
commandment is, that however the breakers
of this commandment may escape
punishment from men, yet the Lord our God
will not suffer them to escape His righteous
judgment (1 Samuel 2:12, 17, 22, 29; 3:13;
Deuteronomy 28:58, 59).

62. What is the fourth commandment?

The fourth commandment is, Remember the Sabbath day to keep it holy: six days shalt thou labor and do all thy work; but the seventh day is the Sabbath of the Lord thy God, in it thou shalt not do any work, thou, nor thy son, nor thy daughter, nor thy man-servant, nor thy maid-servant, nor thy cattle, nor the stranger that is within thy gates: for in six days the Lord made heaven and earth, the sea, and all that in them is, and rested the seventh day; wherefore the Lord blessed the Sabbath day and hallowed it (Exodus 20:8–11).

63. What is required in the fourth commandment?

The fourth commandment requireth the keeping holy to God such set times as He hath appointed in His Word, expressly, one whole day in seven to be a holy sabbath to Himself (Exodus 20:8–11; Deuteronomy 5:12–14).

64. Which day of the seven hath God appointed to be the weekly Sabbath?

Before the resurrection of Christ, God appointed the seventh day of the week to be the weekly Sabbath (Exodus 20:8–11; Deuteronomy 5:12–14); and the first day of the week ever since, to continue to the end of the world, which is the Christian Sabbath (Psalm 118:24; Matthew 28:1; Mark 2:27, 28; John 20:19, 20, 26; Revelation 1:10; Mark 16:2; Luke 24:1, 30–36; John 20:1; Acts 1:3; 2:1, 2; 20:7; 1 Corinthians 16:1, 2).

65. How is the Sabbath to be sanctified?

The Sabbath is to be sanctified by a holy resting all that day (Exodus 20:8, 10), even from such worldly employments and recreations as are lawful on other days (Exodus 16:25–28; Nehemiah 13:15–22); and spending the whole time in the public and private exercises of God's worship (Luke 4:16; Acts 20:7; Psalm 92 title; Isaiah 66:23), except so much as is to be taken up in the works of necessity and mercy (Matthew 12:1–13).

66. What is forbidden in the fourth commandment?
The fourth commandment forbiddeth the omission or careless performance of the duties required (Ezekiel 22:26; Amos 8:5; Malachi 1:13), and the profaning the day by idleness (Acts 20:7, 9), or doing that which is in itself sinful (Ezekiel 23:38), or by unnecessary thoughts, words, or works, about worldly employments or recreations (Jeremiah 17:24–27; Isaiah 58:13).

67. What are the reasons annexed to the fourth commandment?
The reasons annexed to the fourth commandment, are God's allowing us six days of the week for our own lawful employments (Exodus 20:9), His challenging a special propriety in a seventh, His own example, and His blessing the Sabbath day (Exodus 20:11).

68. Which is the fifth commandment?
The fifth commandment is, Honor thy father and thy mother; that thy days may be long in the land which the Lord thy God giveth thee (Exodus 20:12).

69. What is required in the fifth commandment?
The fifth commandment requireth the preserving the honor and performing the duties belonging to everyone in their several places and relations, as superiors (Ephesians 5:21), inferiors (1 Peter 2:17), or equals (Romans 12:10).

70. What is forbidden in the fifth commandment?
The fifth commandment forbiddeth the neglect of, or doing anything against the honor and duty which belongeth to everyone in their several places and relations (Matthew 15:4–6; Ezekiel 34:24; Romans 13:8).

71. What is the reason annexed to the fifth commandment?
The reason annexed to the fifth commandment is a promise of long life and prosperity (as far as it shall serve for God's glory, and their own good) to all such as keep this commandment (Deuteronomy 5:16; Ephesians 6:2, 3).

72. What is the sixth commandment?
The sixth commandment is, Thou shalt not kill (Exodus 20:13).

73. What is required in the sixth commandment?
The sixth commandment requireth all lawful endeavors to preserve our own life (Ephesians 5:28,29) and the life of others (1 Kings 18:4).

74. What is forbidden in the sixth commandment?
The sixth commandment absolutely forbiddeth the taking away of our own life, or the life of our neighbor unjustly, or whatsoever tendeth thereunto (Acts 26:28; Genesis 9:9).

75. Which is the seventh commandment?
The seventh commandment is, Thou shalt not commit adultery (Exodus 20:14).

76. What is required in the seventh commandment?
The seventh commandment requireth the preservation of our own and our neighbor's chastity, in heart, speech, and behavior (1 Corinthians 7:2, 3, 5, 34, 36; Colossians 4:6; 1 Peter 3:2).

77. What is forbidden in the seventh commandment?
The seventh commandment forbiddeth all unchaste thoughts, words, and actions (Matthew 15:19, 5:28; Ephesians 5:3, 4).

78. Which is the eighth commandment?
The eighth commandment is, Thou shalt not steal (Exodus 20:15).

79. What is required in the eighth commandment?
    The eighth commandment requireth the lawful procuring and furthering the wealth and outward estate of ourselves and others (Genesis 30:30; 1 Timothy 5:8; Leviticus 25:35; Deuteronomy 22:1, 2, 3, 4, 5; Exodus 23:4, 5; Genesis 47:14, 20).

80. What is forbidden in the eighth commandment?
    The eighth commandment forbiddeth whatsoever doth or may unjustly hinder our own (1 Timothy 5:8; Proverbs 28:19) or our neighbor's wealth or outward estate (Proverbs 21:17, and 23:20, 21; Ephesians 4:28).

81. Which is the ninth commandment?
    The ninth commandment is, Thou shalt not bear false witness against thy neighbor (Exodus 20:16).

82. What is required in the ninth commandment?
    The ninth commandment requireth the maintaining and promoting of truth between man and man (Zechariah 8:16), and of our own neighbor's good name (John 5:12), especially in witnessbearing (Proverbs 14:5, 25).

83. What is forbidden in the ninth commandment?
The ninth commandment forbiddeth whatsoever is prejudicial to the truth, or injurious to our own or our neighbor's good name (1 Samuel 17:28; Leviticus 19:16; Psalm 15:2, 3).

84. Which is the tenth commandment?
The tenth commandment is Thou shalt not covet thy neighbor's house, thou shalt not covet thy neighbor's wife, nor his man-servant, nor his maid-servant, nor his ox, nor his ass, nor anything that is thy neighbor's (Exodus 20:17).

85. What is required in the tenth commandment?
The tenth commandment requireth full contentment with our own condition (Hebrews 13:5; 1 Timothy 6:6), with a right and charitable frame of spirit toward our neighbor, and all that is his (Job 31:29; Romans 7:15; 1 Timothy 1:5; 1 Corinthians 8:4, 7).

86. What is forbidden in the tenth commandment?
The tenth commandment forbiddeth all discontentment with our own estate (1 Kings 21:4; Esther 5:13; 1 Corinthians 10:10), envying or grieving at the good of our neighbor (Galatians 5:26; James 3:14, 16), and all inordinate motions and affections to anything that is his (Romans 7:7, 8, 13:9; Deuteronomy 5:21).

87. Is. any man able perfectly to keep the commandments of God?
No mere man since the fall is able in this life perfectly to keep the commandments of God (Ecclesiastes 7:20; 1 John 1:8, 10; Galatians 5:17), but doth daily break them in thought, word, or deed (Genesis 4:5, and 7:21; Romans 3:9–21; James 3:2–13).

88. Are all transgressions of the law equally heinous?
Some sins in themselves, and by reason of several aggravations, are more heinous in the sight of God than others (Ezekiel 8:6, 13, 15; 1 John 5:16; Psalm 78:17, 32, 56).

89. What doth every sin deserve?
Every sin deserveth God's wrath and curse, both in this life and that which is to come (Ephesians 5:6; Galatians 3:10; Lamentations 3:39; Matthew 25:41; Romans 6:23).

90. What doth God require of us that we may escape His wrath and curse, due to us for sin?
To escape the wrath and curse of God due to us for sin, God requireth of us faith in Jesus Christ, repentance unto life (Acts 20:21), with the diligent use of all the outward means whereby Christ communicateth to us the benefits of redemption (Proverbs 2:1–6, 8:33 to the end; Isaiah 55:2, 3).

91. What is faith in Jesus Christ?
    Faith in Jesus Christ is a saving grace
    (Hebrews 10:39), whereby we receive and
    rest upon Him alone for salvation, as He is
    offered to us in the gospel (John 1:12; Isaiah
    26:3, 4; Philippians 3:9; Galatians 2:16).

92. What is repentance unto life?
    Repentance unto life is a saving grace (Acts
    11:28), whereby a sinner, out of a true sense
    of his sin (Acts 2:37, 38), and apprehension
    of the mercy of God in Christ (Joel 2:12;
    Jeremiah 3:22), doth, with grief and hatred of
    his sin, turn from it unto God (Jeremiah
    31:18, 19; Ezekiel 36:31), with full purpose of
    and endeavor after new obedience (2
    Corinthians 7:11; Isaiah 1: 16, 17).

93. What are the outward means whereby Christ
    communicateth to us the benefits of
    redemption?
    The outward and ordinary means whereby
    Christ communicateth to us the benefits of
    redemption are his ordinances, especially the
    Word, baptism, the Lord's supper, and
    prayer; all which means are made effectual
    to the elect for salvation (Matthew 28:19, 20;
    Acts 2:42, 46, 47).

94. How is the Word made effectual to salvation?

The Spirit of God maketh the reading, but especially the preaching of the Word, an effectual means of convincing and converting sinners, and of building them up in holiness and comfort through faith unto salvation (Nehemiah 8:8; Acts 26:18; Psalm 19:8; Acts 20:32; Romans 1: 15, 16, 10:13, 14, 15, 16, 17; 15:4; 1 Corinthians 14:24, 25; 2 Timothy 3:15, 16, 17).

95. How is the Word to be read and heard, that it may become effectual to salvation?

That the Word may become effectual to salvation, we must attend thereunto with diligence (Proverbs 8:34), preparation (1 Peter 2:1, 2), and prayer (Psalm 119:18); receive it with faith and love (Hebrews 4:2; 2 Thessalonians 2:10), lay it up in our hearts (Psalm 119:18), and practice it in our lives (Luke 8:15; James 1:25).

96. How do baptism and the Lords supper become effectual means of salvation?

Baptism and the Lords supper become effectual means of salvation, not any virtue in them, or in him that doth administer them, but only by the blessing of Christ (1 Peter 3:21; Matthew 3:11; 1 Corinthians 3:6, 7), and the working of the Spirit in those that by faith receive them (1 Corinthians 12:3; Matthew 28:19).

97. What is baptism?

Baptism is an ordinance of the New Testament instituted by Jesus Christ, to be unto the party baptized a sign of his fellowship with Him, in His death, burial, and resurrection; of his being ingrafted into Him (Romans 6:3, 4, 5; Colossians 2:12; Galatians 3:27); of remission of sins (Mark 1:4; Acts 2:38, and 22:16); and of his giving up himself unto God through Jesus Christ, to live and walk in newness of life (Romans 6:3, 4).

98. To whom is baptism to be administered?

Baptism is to be administered to all those who actually profess repentance towards God (Acts 2:38; Matthew 3:6), faith in and obedience to our Lord Jesus Christ, and to none other (Acts 8:12, 36, 37, 38; 10:47, 48).

99. Are the infants of such as are professing believers to be baptized?

The infants of such as are professing believers are not to be baptized, because there is neither command or example in the holy Scriptures, or certain consequence from them to baptize such (Exodus 23:13; Proverbs 30:6; Luke 3:7, 8).

100. How is Baptism rightly administered?

Baptism is rightly administered by immersion, or dipping the whole body of the party in water, into the name of the Father, and of the Son, and of the Holy Spirit, according to Christ's institution, and the practice of the apostles (Matthew 3:16; John 3:23; 4:1, 2; Matthew 28:19, 20; Acts 8:38; Romans 6:4; Colossians 2:12), and not by sprinkling or pouring of water, or dipping some part of the body, after the tradition of men.

101. What is the duty of such who are rightly baptized?

It is the duty of such who are rightly baptized to give up themselves to some particular and orderly church of Jesus Christ, that they may walk in all the commandments and ordinances of the Lord blameless (Acts 2:41, 42; 5:13, 14; 9:26; 1 Peter 2:5; Luke 1:6).

102. What is the Lord's supper?

The Lord's supper is an ordinance of the New Testament, instituted by Jesus Christ; wherein by giving and receiving bread and wine, according to His appointment, His death is shown forth, and the worthy receivers are, not after a corporal and carnal manner, but by faith, made partakers of His body and blood, with all His benefits, to their spiritual nourishment and growth in grace (Matthew 26:26, 27, 28; 1 Corinthians 11:23–26; 10:16).

103. Who are the proper subjects of this ordinance?
They who have been baptized upon a personal profession of their faith in Jesus Christ, and repentance from dead works (Acts 2:41, 42).

104. What is required to the worthy receiving of the Lord's supper?
It is required of them that would worthily partake of the Lord's supper, that they examine themselves of their knowledge to discern the Lord's body (1 Corinthians 11:28, 29), of their faith to feed upon Him (2 Corinthians 13:5), of their repentance (1 Corinthians 11:31), love (1 Corinthians 10:16, 17), and new obedience (1 Corinthians 5:7, 8), lest coming unworthily they eat and drink judgment to themselves (1 Corinthians 11:28, 29).

105. What is prayer?
Prayer is an offering up our desires to God (Psalm 62:8), by the assistance of the Holy Spirit (Romans 8:26), for things agreeable to His will (1 John 5:14; Romans 8:27), in the name of Christ (John 16:23), believing (Matthew 21:22; James 1:6), with confession of our sins (Psalm 32:5, 6; Daniel 9:4), and thankful acknowledgments of His mercies (Philippians 4:6).

106. What rule hath God given for our direction in prayer?

The whole Word of God is of use to direct us in prayer (1 John 5:14); but the special rule of direction is that prayer which Christ taught His disciples, commonly called the Lord's prayer (Matthew 6:9–13; with Luke 11:2–4).

107. What doth the preface of the Lord's prayer teach us?

The preface of the Lord's prayer, which is Our Father which art in heaven (Matthew 6:9), teacheth us to draw near to God with all holy reverence and confidence, as children to a father, able and ready to help us (Romans 8:15; Luke 11:13; Isaiah 24:8); and that we should pray with and for others (Acts 12:5; 1 Timothy 2:1, 2).

108. What do we pray for in the first petition?

In the first petition, which is, Hallowed be Thy name (Matthew 6:9), we pray that God would enable us and others to glorify Him in all that whereby He maketh Himself known (Psalm 67:2, 3), and that He would dispose all things to His own glory (Psalm 83 throughout; Romans 11:36).

109. What do we pray for in the second petition?
In the second petition, which is, Thy kingdom come (Matthew 6:10), we pray that Satan's kingdom may be destroyed (Psalm 68:1, 18), and that the kingdom of grace may be advanced (Revelation 12:10, 11), ourselves and others brought into it and kept in it (2 Thessalonians 3: 1; Romans 10: 1; John 17:19, 20), and that the kingdom of glory may be hastened (Revelation 22:10).

110. What do we pray for in the third petition?
In the third petition, which is, Thy will be done on earth as it is in heaven (Matthew 6:10), we pray that God by His grace would make us able and willing to know, obey, and submit to His will in all things (Psalm 67: throughout; Psalm 119:36; 2 Samuel 15:25; Job 1:21), as the angels do in heaven (Psalm 103:20, 21).

111. What do we pray for in the fourth petition?
In the fourth petition, which is, Give us this day our daily bread (Matthew 6:11), we pray that of God's free gift we may receive a competent portion of the good things of this life, and enjoy His blessing with them (Proverbs 30:8; Genesis 28:20; 1 Timothy 4:4, 5).

112. What do we pray for in the fifth petition?

In the fifth petition, which is, And forgive us our debts as we forgive our debtors (Matthew 6:12), we pray that God, for Christ's sake, would freely pardon all our sins (Psalm 51:1, 2, 7, 9; Daniel 9:17–19); which we are rather encouraged to ask because of His grace we are enabled from the heart to forgive others (Luke 11:4; Matthew 18:35).

113. What do we pray for in the sixth petition?

In the sixth petition, which is, And lead us not into temptation but deliver us from evil (Matthew 6:13), we pray that God would either keep us from being tempted to sin (Matthew 26:31), or support and deliver us when we are tempted (2 Corinthians 12:8).

114. What doth the conclusion of the Lord's prayer teach?

The conclusion of the Lord's prayer, which is, For Thine is the kingdom, and the power, and the glory, forever. Amen (Matthew 6:13), teacheth us to take our encouragement in prayer from God only (Daniel 9:4, 7–9, 16–19), and in our prayers to praise Him, ascribing kingdom, power, and glory, to Him (1 Chronicles 29:10–13). And in testimony of our desire and assurance to be heard, we say, Amen (1 Corinthians 4:16; Revelation 11:20; 22:20, 21).

❝

The Scriptures of God are my only fountain and
substance in all matters of weight and importance.

❞

JOHN OWEN

❝

The Bible in memory is better than the Bible
in the book case.

❞

C. H. SPURGEON

SCRIPTURE MEMORY

PSALM 103:1–8

Bless the Lord, O my soul,
and all that is within me,
bless his holy name!
Bless the Lord, O my soul,
and forget not all his benefits,
who forgives all your iniquity,
who heals all your diseases,
who redeems your life from the pit,
who crowns you with steadfast love and mercy,
who satisfies you with good
so that your youth is renewed like the eagle's.

The Lord works righteousness
and justice for all who are oppressed.
He made known his ways to Moses,
his acts to the people of Israel.
The Lord is merciful and gracious,
slow to anger and abounding in steadfast love.

ISAIAH 46:9–10

Remember the former things of old;
for I am God, and there is no other;
I am God, and there is none like me,
declaring the end from the beginning
and from ancient times things not yet done,
saying, 'My counsel shall stand,
and I will accomplish all my purpose,'

DEUTERONOMY 29:29

The secret things belong to the Lord our God, but
the things that are revealed belong to us and to our
children forever, that we may do all the words of
this law.

EPHESIANS 1:2–9

Grace to you and peace from God our Father and
the Lord Jesus Christ.

Blessed be the God and Father of our Lord Jesus
Christ, who has blessed us in Christ with every
spiritual blessing in the heavenly places, even as he
chose us in him before the foundation of the world,
that we should be holy and blameless before him. In
love he predestined us for adoption to himself as
sons through Jesus Christ, according to the purpose
of his will, to the praise of his glorious grace, with
which he has blessed us in the Beloved. In him we
have redemption through his blood, the forgiveness
of our trespasses, according to the riches of his grace,
which he lavished upon us, in all wisdom and
insight making known to us the mystery of his will,
according to his purpose, which he set forth in Christ

PROVERBS 6:16–19

There are six things that the Lord hates,
seven that are an abomination to him:
haughty eyes, a lying tongue,
and hands that shed innocent blood,
a heart that devises wicked plans,
feet that make haste to run to evil,
a false witness who breathes out lies,
and one who sows discord among brothers.

PROVERBS 18:24

A man of many companions may come to ruin,
but there is a friend who sticks closer than a
brother.

HEBREWS 11:6

And without faith it is impossible to please him,
for whoever would draw near to God must believe
that he exists and that he rewards those who seek
him.

PSALM 119:41–56

Waw

Let your steadfast love come to me, O Lord,
your salvation according to your promise;
then shall I have an answer for him who taunts me,
for I trust in your word.
And take not the word of truth utterly out of my
mouth,
for my hope is in your rules.
I will keep your law continually,
forever and ever,

and I shall walk in a wide place,
for I have sought your precepts.
I will also speak of your testimonies before kings
and shall not be put to shame,
for I find my delight in your commandments,
which I love.
I will lift up my hands toward your
commandments, which I love,
and I will meditate on your statutes.

Zayin
Remember your word to your servant,
in which you have made me hope.
This is my comfort in my affliction,
that your promise gives me life.
The insolent utterly deride me,
but I do not turn away from your law.
When I think of your rules from of old,
I take comfort, O Lord.
Hot indignation seizes me because of the wicked,
who forsake your law.
Your statutes have been my songs
in the house of my sojourning.
I remember your name in the night, O Lord,
and keep your law.
This blessing has fallen to me,
that I have kept your precepts.

EXODUS 20:1-17 (THE TEN COMMANDMENTS)

And God spoke all these words, saying,

"I am the Lord your God, who brought you out of the land of Egypt, out of the house of slavery.

"You shall have no other gods before me.

"You shall not make for yourself a carved image, or any likeness of anything that is in heaven above, or that is in the earth beneath, or that is in the water under the earth. You shall not bow down to them or serve them, for I the Lord your God am a jealous God, visiting the iniquity of the fathers on the children to the third and the fourth generation of those who hate me, but showing steadfast love to thousands of those who love me and keep my commandments.

"You shall not take the name of the Lord your God in vain, for the Lord will not hold him guiltless who takes his name in vain.

"Remember the Sabbath day, to keep it holy. Six days you shall labor, and do all your work, but the seventh day is a Sabbath to the Lord your God. On it you shall not do any work, you, or your son, or your daughter, your male servant, or your female servant, or your livestock, or the sojourner who is within your gates. For in six days the Lord made heaven and earth, the sea, and all that is in them, and rested on the seventh day. Therefore the Lord blessed the Sabbath day and made it holy.

"Honor your father and your mother, that your days may be long in the land that the Lord your God is giving you.

"You shall not murder.

"You shall not commit adultery.

"You shall not steal.

"You shall not bear false witness against your neighbor.

"You shall not covet your neighbor's house; you shall not covet your neighbor's wife, or his male servant, or his female servant, or his ox, or his donkey, or anything that is your neighbor's."

JOHN 14:1–7

"Let not your hearts be troubled. Believe in God; believe also in me. In my Father's house are many rooms. If it were not so, would I have told you that I go to prepare a place for you? And if I go and prepare a place for you, I will come again and will take you to myself, that where I am you may be also. And you know the way to where I am going." Thomas said to him, "Lord, we do not know where you are going. How can we know the way?" Jesus said to him, "I am the way, and the truth, and the life. No one comes to the Father except through me. If you had known me, you would have known my Father also. From now on you do know him and have seen him."

MATTHEW 22:36–40

"Teacher, which is the great commandment in the Law?" And he said to him, "You shall love the Lord your God with all your heart and with all your soul and with all your mind. This is the great and first commandment. And a second is like it: You shall love your neighbor as yourself. On these two commandments depend all the Law and the Prophets."

MARK 10:45

For even the Son of Man came not to be served but to serve, and to give his life as a ransom for many.

1 CORINTHIANS 13

If I speak in the tongues of men and of angels, but have not love, I am a noisy gong or a clanging cymbal. And if I have prophetic powers, and understand all mysteries and all knowledge, and if I have all faith, so as to remove mountains, but have not love, I am nothing. If I give away all I have, and if I deliver up my body to be burned, but have not love, I gain nothing.

Love is patient and kind; love does not envy or boast; it is not arrogant or rude. It does not insist on its own way; it is not irritable or resentful; it does not rejoice at wrongdoing, but rejoices with the truth. Love bears all things, believes all things, hopes all things, endures all things.

Love never ends. As for prophecies, they will pass away; as for tongues, they will cease; as for knowledge, it will pass away. For we know in part and we prophesy in part, but when the perfect comes, the partial will pass away. When I was a child, I spoke like a child, I thought like a child, I reasoned like a child. When I became a man, I gave up childish ways. For now we see in a mirror dimly, but then face to face. Now I know in part; then I shall know fully, even as I have been fully known.

So now faith, hope, and love abide, these three; but the greatest of these is love.

ECCLESIASTES 12:13–14

The end of the matter; all has been heard. Fear God and keep his commandments, for this is the whole duty of man. For God will bring every deed into judgment, with every secret thing, whether good or evil.

PSALM 119:57–80

Heth
  The Lord is my portion;
  I promise to keep your words.
  I entreat your favor with all my heart;
  be gracious to me according to your promise.
  When I think on my ways,
  I turn my feet to your testimonies;
  I hasten and do not delay
  to keep your commandments.
  Though the cords of the wicked ensnare me,
  I do not forget your law.
  At midnight I rise to praise you,
  because of your righteous rules.
  I am a companion of all who fear you,
  of those who keep your precepts.
  The earth, O Lord, is full of your steadfast love;
  teach me your statutes!

Teth
  You have dealt well with your servant,
  O Lord, according to your word.
  Teach me good judgment and knowledge,
  for I believe in your commandments.
  Before I was afflicted I went astray,

but now I keep your word.
You are good and do good;
teach me your statutes.
The insolent smear me with lies,
but with my whole heart I keep your precepts;
their heart is unfeeling like fat,
but I delight in your law.
It is good for me that I was afflicted,
that I might learn your statutes.
The law of your mouth is better to me
than thousands of gold and silver pieces.

Yodh
Your hands have made and fashioned me;
give me understanding that I may learn your
commandments.
Those who fear you shall see me and rejoice,
because I have hoped in your word.
I know, O Lord, that your rules are righteous,
and that in faithfulness you have afflicted me.
Let your steadfast love comfort me
according to your promise to your servant.
Let your mercy come to me, that I may live;
for your law is my delight.
Let the insolent be put to shame,
because they have wronged me with falsehood;
as for me, I will meditate on your precepts.
Let those who fear you turn to me,
that they may know your testimonies.
May my heart be blameless in your statutes,
that I may not be put to shame!

JOHN 15:16

You did not choose me, but I chose you and appointed you that you should go and bear fruit and that your fruit should abide, so that whatever you ask the Father in my name, he may give it to you.

JOHN 17:9–11

I am praying for them. I am not praying for the world but for those whom you have given me, for they are yours. All mine are yours, and yours are mine, and I am glorified in them. And I am no longer in the world, but they are in the world, and I am coming to you. Holy Father, keep them in your name, which you have given me, that they may be one, even as we are one.

ROMANS 8:29–30

For those whom he foreknew he also predestined to be conformed to the image of his Son, in order that he might be the firstborn among many brothers. And those whom he predestined he also called, and those whom he called he also justified, and those whom he justified he also glorified.

PROVERBS 21:23

Whoever keeps his mouth and his tongue
keeps himself out of trouble.

PROVERBS 16:32

Whoever is slow to anger is better than the mighty,
and he who rules his spirit than he who takes a city.

PROVERBS 23:23

Buy truth, and do not sell it;
buy wisdom, instruction, and understanding.

PSALM 27

The Lord is my light and my salvation;
whom shall I fear?
The Lord is the stronghold of my life;
of whom shall I be afraid?

When evildoers assail me
to eat up my flesh,
my adversaries and foes,
it is they who stumble and fall.

Though an army encamp against me,
my heart shall not fear;
though war arise against me,
yet I will be confident.

One thing have I asked of the Lord,
that will I seek after:
that I may dwell in the house of the Lord
all the days of my life,
to gaze upon the beauty of the Lord
and to inquire in his temple.

For he will hide me in his shelter
in the day of trouble;

he will conceal me under the cover of his tent;
he will lift me high upon a rock.

And now my head shall be lifted up
above my enemies all around me,
and I will offer in his tent
sacrifices with shouts of joy;
I will sing and make melody to the Lord.

Hear, O Lord, when I cry aloud;
be gracious to me and answer me!
You have said, "Seek my face."
My heart says to you,
"Your face, Lord, do I seek."
Hide not your face from me.
Turn not your servant away in anger,
O you who have been my help.
Cast me not off; forsake me not,
O God of my salvation!
For my father and my mother have forsaken me,
but the Lord will take me in.

Teach me your way, O Lord,
and lead me on a level path
because of my enemies.
Give me not up to the will of my adversaries;
for false witnesses have risen against me,
and they breathe out violence.

I believe that I shall look upon the goodness of the
Lord
in the land of the living!
Wait for the Lord;

be strong, and let your heart take courage;
wait for the Lord!

PSALM 119:81–112
Kaph
  My soul longs for your salvation;
  I hope in your word.
  My eyes long for your promise;
  I ask, "When will you comfort me?"
  For I have become like a wineskin in the smoke,
  yet I have not forgotten your statutes.
  How long must your servant endure?
  When will you judge those who persecute me?
  The insolent have dug pitfalls for me;
  they do not live according to your law.
  All your commandments are sure;
  they persecute me with falsehood; help me!
  They have almost made an end of me on earth,
  but I have not forsaken your precepts.
  In your steadfast love give me life,
  that I may keep the testimonies of your mouth.

Lamedh
  Forever, O Lord, your word
  is firmly fixed in the heavens.
  Your faithfulness endures to all generations;
  you have established the earth, and it stands fast.
  By your appointment they stand this day,
  for all things are your servants.
  If your law had not been my delight,
  I would have perished in my affliction.
  I will never forget your precepts,
  for by them you have given me life.

I am yours; save me,
for I have sought your precepts.
The wicked lie in wait to destroy me,
but I consider your testimonies.
I have seen a limit to all perfection,
but your commandment is exceedingly broad.

Mem

Oh how I love your law!
It is my meditation all the day.
Your commandment makes me wiser than my
enemies,
for it is ever with me.
I have more understanding than all my teachers,
for your testimonies are my meditation.
I understand more than the aged,
for I keep your precepts.
I hold back my feet from every evil way,
in order to keep your word.
I do not turn aside from your rules,
for you have taught me.
How sweet are your words to my taste,
sweeter than honey to my mouth!
Through your precepts I get understanding;
therefore I hate every false way.

Nun

Your word is a lamp to my feet
and a light to my path.
I have sworn an oath and confirmed it,
to keep your righteous rules.
I am severely afflicted;
give me life, O Lord, according to your word!

Accept my freewill offerings of praise, O Lord,
and teach me your rules.
I hold my life in my hand continually,
but I do not forget your law.
The wicked have laid a snare for me,
but I do not stray from your precepts.
Your testimonies are my heritage forever,
for they are the joy of my heart.
I incline my heart to perform your statutes
forever, to the end.

PHILIPPIANS 2:5–13

Have this mind among yourselves, which is yours in Christ Jesus, who, though he was in the form of God, did not count equality with God a thing to be grasped, but emptied himself, by taking the form of a servant, being born in the likeness of men. And being found in human form, he humbled himself by becoming obedient to the point of death, even death on a cross. Therefore God has highly exalted him and bestowed on him the name that is above every name, so that at the name of Jesus every knee should bow, in heaven and on earth and under the earth, and every tongue confess that Jesus Christ is Lord, to the glory of God the Father.

Therefore, my beloved, as you have always obeyed, so now, not only as in my presence but much more in my absence, work out your own salvation with fear and trembling, for it is God who works in you, both to will and to work for his good pleasure.

GALATIANS 2:16

Yet we know that a person is not justified by works of the law but through faith in Jesus Christ, so we also have believed in Christ Jesus, in order to be justified by faith in Christ and not by works of the law, because by works of the law no one will be justified.

EPHESIANS 2:8–10

For by grace you have been saved through faith. And this is not your own doing; it is the gift of God, not a result of works, so that no one may boast. For we are his workmanship, created in Christ Jesus for good works, which God prepared beforehand, that we should walk in them.

2 CORINTHIANS 12:9

But he said to me, "My grace is sufficient for you, for my power is made perfect in weakness." Therefore I will boast all the more gladly of my weaknesses, so that the power of Christ may rest upon me.

ISAIAH 26:3–4

You keep him in perfect peace
whose mind is stayed on you,
because he trusts in you.
Trust in the Lord forever,
for the Lord God is an everlasting rock.

PROVERBS 15:5

A fool despises his father's instruction,
but whoever heeds reproof is prudent.

PSALM 119:113–136
Samekh
>I hate the double-minded,
>but I love your law.
>You are my hiding place and my shield;
>I hope in your word.
>Depart from me, you evildoers,
>that I may keep the commandments of my God.
>Uphold me according to your promise, that I may live,
>and let me not be put to shame in my hope!
>Hold me up, that I may be safe
>and have regard for your statutes continually!
>You spurn all who go astray from your statutes,
>for their cunning is in vain.
>All the wicked of the earth you discard like dross,
>therefore I love your testimonies.
>My flesh trembles for fear of you,
>and I am afraid of your judgments.

Ayin
>I have done what is just and right;
>do not leave me to my oppressors.
>Give your servant a pledge of good;
>let not the insolent oppress me.
>My eyes long for your salvation
>and for the fulfillment of your righteous promise.
>Deal with your servant according to your steadfast love,
>and teach me your statutes.
>I am your servant; give me understanding,
>that I may know your testimonies!

It is time for the Lord to act,
for your law has been broken.
Therefore I love your commandments
above gold, above fine gold.
Therefore I consider all your precepts to be right;
I hate every false way.

Pe

Your testimonies are wonderful;
therefore my soul keeps them.
The unfolding of your words gives light;
it imparts understanding to the simple.
I open my mouth and pant,
because I long for your commandments.
Turn to me and be gracious to me,
as is your way with those who love your name.
Keep steady my steps according to your promise,
and let no iniquity get dominion over me.
Redeem me from man's oppression,
that I may keep your precepts.
Make your face shine upon your servant,
and teach me your statutes.
My eyes shed streams of tears,
because people do not keep your law.

SCRIPTURE MEMORY

ISAIAH 55:6–11

"Seek the Lord while he may be found;
call upon him while he is near;
let the wicked forsake his way,
and the unrighteous man his thoughts;
let him return to the Lord, that he may have
compassion on him,
and to our God, for he will abundantly pardon.
For my thoughts are not your thoughts,
neither are your ways my ways, declares the Lord.
For as the heavens are higher than the earth,
so are my ways higher than your ways
and my thoughts than your thoughts.

"For as the rain and the snow come down from heaven
and do not return there but water the earth,
making it bring forth and sprout,
giving seed to the sower and bread to the eater,
so shall my word be that goes out from my mouth;
it shall not return to me empty,
but it shall accomplish that which I purpose,
and shall succeed in the thing for which I sent it."

66

Always stand to it that your creed must bend
to the Bible, and not the Bible to your creed.

99

C. H. SPURGEON

66

Children are not a distraction from more important
work, they are the most important work.

99

C. S. LEWIS

BIBLE BASICS

THE TEN COMMANDMENTS
Summarized Version

1. You shall have no other gods before me.
2. You shall not make for yourself any carved image.
3. You shall not take the name of the LORD your God in vain.
4. Remember the Sabbath day, to keep it holy.
5. Honor your father and mother.
6. You shall not murder.
7. You shall not commit adultery.
8. You shall not steal.
9. You shall not bear false witness.
10. You shall not covet.

THE LORD'S PRAYER
Matthew 6:9-13

Pray then like this:
"Our Father in heaven,
hallowed be your name.
Your kingdom come,
your will be done,
on earth as it is in heaven.
Give us this day our daily bread,
and forgive us our debts,
as we also have forgiven our debtors.
And lead us not into temptation,
but deliver us from evil.

NAMES OF THE TWELVE APOSTLES

1. Simon Peter
2. Andrew
3. James (son of Zebedee)
4. John (son of Zebedee)
5. Philip
6. Bartholomew
7. Matthew
8. Thomas
9. James (son of Alphaeus)
10. Simon
11. Thaddaeus (Judas, son of James)
12. Judas Iscariot

THE APOSTLES' CREED

I believe in God, the Father Almighty,
the Maker of heaven and earth,
and in Jesus Christ, His only Son, our Lord:
Who was conceived by the Holy Ghost,
born of the virgin Mary,
suffered under Pontius Pilate,
was crucified, dead, and buried;
He descended into hell.
The third day He arose again from the dead;
He ascended into heaven,
and sitteth on the right hand of God the Father
Almighty;
from thence he shall come to judge the quick and
the dead.
I believe in the Holy Ghost;
the holy catholic church;
the communion of saints;
the forgiveness of sins;
the resurrection of the body;
and the life everlasting.
Amen.

(NOTE: The meaning of "catholic" is not to be
confused with the Roman Catholic Church. It
means universal.)

THE BOOKS OF THE BIBLE

Old Testament		
Genesis	II Chronicles	Daniel
Exodus	Ezra	Hosea
Leviticus	Nehemiah	Joel
Numbers	Esther	Amos
Deuteronomy	Job	Obadiah
Joshua	Psalm	Jonah
Judges	Proverbs	Micah
Ruth	Ecclesiastes	Nahum
I Samuel	Song of Solomon	Habakkuk
II Samuel	Isaiah	Zephaniah
I Kings	Jeremiah	Haggai
II Kings	Lamentations	Zechariah
I Chronicles	Ezekiel	Malachi

New Testament		
Matthew	Ephesians	Hebrews
Mark	Philippians	James
Luke	Colossians	I Peter
John	I Thessalonians	II Peter
Acts	II Thessalonians	I John
Romans	I Timothy	II John
I Corinthians	II Timothy	III John
II Corinthians	Titus	Jude
Galatians	Philemon	Revelation

THE NICENE CREED

I believe in one God, the Father Almighty, Maker of heaven and earth, and of all things visible and invisible.

And in one Lord Jesus Christ, the only-begotten Son of God, begotten of the Father before all worlds; God of God, Light of Light, very God of very God; begotten, not made, being of one substance with the Father, by whom all things were made.

Who, for us men and for our salvation, came down from heaven, and was incarnate by the Holy Spirit of the virgin Mary, and was made man; and was crucified also for us under Pontius Pilate; He suffered and was buried; and the third day He rose again, according to the Scriptures; and ascended into heaven, and sits on the right hand of the Father; and He shall come again, with glory, to judge the quick and the dead; whose kingdom shall have no end.

And I believe in the Holy Ghost, the Lord and Giver of Life; who proceeds from the Father and the Son; who with the Father and the Son together is worshipped and glorified; who spoke by the prophets.

And I believe in one holy catholic and apostolic Church. I acknowledge one baptism for the remission of sins; and I look for the resurrection of the dead, and the life of the world to come. Amen.

"

Beautiful music is the art of the prophets that can calm the agitations of the soul; it is one of the most magnificent and delightful presents God has given us.

"

MARTIN LUTHER

"

The foundation of worship in the heart is not emotional it is theological.

"

SINCLAIR FERGUSON

HYMNS

THE CHURCH'S ONE FOUNDATION
Words by Samuel J. Stone (1866)

Verse 1

The church's one foundation
Is Jesus Christ her Lord;
She is His new creation,
By Spirit and the Word:
From heaven He came and sought her
To be His holy bride,
With His own blood He bought her,
And for her life He died.

Verse 2

Elect from every nation,
Yet one o'er all the earth,
Her charter of salvation,
One Lord, one faith, one birth;
One holy name she blesses,
Partakes one holy food,
And to one hope she presses,
With every grace endued.

Verse 3

Though with a scornful wonder
The world see her oppressed,
By schisms rent asunder,
By heresies distressed,
Yet saints their watch are keeping;
Their cry goes up: "How long?"
And soon the night of weeping
Shall be the morn of song.

Verse 4

Yet she on earth hath union
With God the Three and One,
And mystic sweet communion
With those whose rest is won:
O happy ones and holy!
Lord, give us grace that we,
Like them, the meek and lowly,
On high may dwell with Thee.
Amen.

WHEN I SURVEY THE WONDROUS CROSS
Words by Isaac Watts (1707)

Verse 1

When I survey the wondrous cross,
On which the Prince of glory died,
My richest gain I count but loss,
And pour contempt on all my pride.

Verse 2

Forbid it, Lord, that I should boast,
Save in the death of Christ my God;
All the vain things that charm me most,
I sacrifice them to His blood.

Verse 3

See, from His head, His hands, His feet
Sorrow and love flow mingled down;
Did e'er such love and sorrow meet,
Or thorns compose so rich a crown.

Verse 4

Were the whole realm of nature mine,
That were a present far to small;
Love so amazing, so divine,
Demands my soul, my life, my all.
Amen.

HOW SWEET AND AWFUL IS THE PLACE
Words by Isaac Watts (1707)

Verse 1

How sweet and awful is the place
With Christ within the doors,
While everlasting love displays
The choicest of her stores.

Verse 2

While all our hearts and all our songs
Join to admire the feast,
Each of us cry, with thankful tongues,
"Lord, why was I a guest?"

Verse 3

"Why was I made to hear Thy voice
And enter while there's room,
When thousands make a wretched choice,
And rather starve than come?"

Verse 4

'Twas the same love that spread the feast
That sweetly drew us in;
Else we had still refused to taste,
And perished in our sin.

Verse 5

Pity the nations, O our God,
Constrain the earth to come;
Send Thy victorious Word abroad,
And bring the strangers home.

Verse 6
We long to see Thy churches full,
That all the chosen race
May, with one voice and heart and soul,
Sing thy redeeming grace.
Amen.

HALLELUJAH, PRAISE JEHOVAH
From Psalm 146 in The Psalter (1912)

Verse 1

Hallelujah, praise Jehovah,
O my soul, Jehovah praise;
I will sing the glorious praises
Of my God through all my days.
Put no confidence in princes,
Nor for help on man depend;
He shall die, to dust returning,
And his purposes shall end.

Verse 2

Happy is the man that chooses
Israel's God to be his aid;
He is blessed whose hope of blessing
On the Lord his God is stayed.
Heav'n and earth the Lord created,
Seas and all that they contain;
He delivers from oppression,
Righteousness He will maintain.

Verse 3

Food He daily gives the hungry,
Sets the mourning pris'ner free,
Raises those bowed down in anguish,
Makes the sightless eyes to see.
Well Jehovah loves the righteous,
And the stranger He befriends,
Helps the fatherless and widow,
Judgment on the wicked sends.

Verse 4

Hallelujah, praise Jehovah,
O my soul, Jehovah praise;
I will sing the glorious praises
Of my God through all my days.
Over all God reigns forever,
Though all ages He is King;
Unto Him, thy God, O Zion,
Joyful hallelujahs sing.
Amen.

GREAT IS THY FAITHFULNESS
Words by Thomas O. Chisholm (1923)

Verse 1
Great is Thy faithfulness, O God my Father,
There is no shadow of turning with Thee;
Thou changest not, Thy compassions, they fail not;
As Thou hast been Thou forever wilt be.

Refrain
Great is Thy faithfulness!
Great is Thy faithfulness!
Morning by morning new mercies I see;
All I have needed Thy hand hath provided;
Great is Thy faithfulness, Lord, unto me!

Verse 2
Summer and winter, and springtime and harvest,
Sun, moon and stars in their courses above
Join with all nature in manifold witness
To Thy great faithfulness, mercy and love.

Refrain

Verse 3
Pardon for sin and a peace that endureth,
Thine own dear presence to cheer and to guide;
Strength for today and bright hope for tomorrow,
Blessings all mine, with ten thousand beside!

Refrain

Amen.

COME YE SINNERS
Words by Joseph Hart (1759)

Verse 1

Come, ye sinners, poor and wretched,
Weak and wounded, sick and sore;
Jesus ready stands to save you,
Full of pity joined with pow'r:
      He is able,
      He is able,
      He is able,
He is willing; doubt no more.

Verse 2

Come, ye needy, come and welcome,
God's free bounty glorify;
True belief and true repentance,
Ev'ry grace that brings you nigh,
      Without money,
      Without money,
      Without money,
Come to Jesus Christ and buy.

Verse 3

Come, ye weary, heavy laden,
Bruised and broken by the fall;
If you tarry till you're better,
You will never come at all:
      Not the righteous,
      Not the righteous,
      Not the righteous—
Sinners Jesus came to call.

Verse 4

Let not conscience make you linger,
Nor of fitness fondly dream;
All the fitness he requireth
Is to feel your need of Him;
  This He gives you,
  This He gives you,
  This He gives you;
'Tis the Spirit's rising beam.

Verse 5

Lo! th' incarnate God ascended,
Pleads the merit of His blood;
Ventures on Him, venture wholly,
Let no other trust intrude:
  None but Jesus,
  None but Jesus,
  None but Jesus
Can do helpless sinners good.
Amen.

A MIGHTY FORTRESS IS OUR GOD
Words by Martin Luther (1529) From Psalm 46

Verse 1

A mighty fortress is our God,
A bulwark never failing;
Our helper He, amid the flood
Of mortal ills prevailing:
For still our ancient foe
Doth seek to work us woe;
His craft and power are great,
And armed with cruel hate,
On earth is not his equal.

Verse 2

Did we in our own strength confide,
Our striving would be losing;
Were not the right Man on our side,
The Man of God's own choosing:
Dost ask who that may be?
Christ Jesus it is He;
Lord Sabbaoth, His name,
From age to age the same,
And He must win the battle.

Verse 3

And tho' this world, with devils filled,
Should threaten to undo us,
We will not fear, for God hath willed
His truth to triumph through us:

The Prince of Darkness grim—
We tremble not for him;
His rage we can endure,
For lo, his doom is sure,
One little word shall fell him.

Verse 4
That word above all earthly powers,
No thanks to them, abideth;
The Spirit and the gifts are ours
Thro' Him who with us sideth:
Let goods and kindred go,
This mortal life also;
The body they may kill:
God's truth abideth still,
His kingdom is forever.
Amen.

STAND UP, STAND UP FOR JESUS
Words by George Duffield (1858)

Verse 1
Stand up, stand up for Jesus,
Ye soldiers of the cross;
Lift high the royal banner,
It must not suffer loss:
From vict'ry unto vict'ry
His army shall He lead,
Till ev'ry foe is vanquished,
And Christ is Lord indeed.

Verse 2
Stand up, Stand up for Jesus,
Stand in His strength alone;
The arm of flesh will fail you,
Ye dare not trust your own:
Put on the gospel armor,
Each piece put on with prayer;
Where duty calls or danger,
Be never wanting there.

Verse 3
Stand up, stand up for Jesus,
The strife will not be long;
This day the noise of battle,
The next the victor's song:
To him that overcometh
A crown of life shall be;
He, with the King of glory,
Shall reign eternally.
Amen.

"

The word of God can be in the mind without being in the heart, but it cannot be in the heart without first being in the mind.

"

R. C. SPROUL

"

You may speak but a word to a child, and in that child there may be slumbering a noble heart which shall stir the Christian Church in years to come.

"

C. H. SPURGEON

TRACK YOUR PROGRESS

The following is an outline of memory work from Book 2 divided into suggested age. If you are not beginning with age ten, we suggest that you begin with the appropriate Scripture, hymns, etc. for your child, as well as with question #1 of *The Baptist Catechism*. The catechism is written in a systematic format with each question built upon those before it. The memorization of the whole catechism will expose the child to a solid doctrinal foundation.

AGE TEN
The Baptist Catechism

Questions #1-5   Date: _____
Questions #6-10   Date: _____
Questions #11-15   Date: _____
Questions #16-20   Date: _____
Questions #21-25   Date: _____
Questions #26-29   Date: _____

Scriptures

Psalm 103:1–8   Date: _____
Isaiah 46:9–10   Date: _____
Deuteronomy 29:29   Date: _____
Ephesians 1:2–9   Date: _____
Proverbs 6:16–19   Date: _____
Proverbs 18:24   Date: _____
Hebrews 11:6   Date: _____
Psalm 119:41–56   Date: _____
Exodus 20:1–17   Date: _____

Bible Basics

The Ten Commandments   Date: _____
The Lord's Prayer   Date: _____

Hymns

The Church's
One Foundation   Date: _____
When I Survey
the Wondrous Cross   Date: _____

AGE ELEVEN
The Baptist Catechism

Questions #30-35   Date: _____
Questions #36-40   Date: _____
Questions #41-45   Date: _____
Questions #46-50   Date: _____
Questions #51-55   Date: _____
Questions #56-59   Date: _____

Scriptures

John 14:1–7   Date: _____
Matthew 22:36–40   Date: _____
Mark 10:45   Date: _____
1 Corinthians 13   Date: _____
Ecclesiastes 12:13–14   Date: _____
Psalm 119:57–80   Date: _____

Bible Basics

The Names of
the Twelve Apostles   Date: _____

The Apostles' Creed   Date: _____

Hymns

How Sweet and
Awful is the Place   Date: _____
Hallelujah,
Praise Jehovah   Date: _____

AGE TWELVE
The Baptist Catechism

Questions #60-64   Date: _____
Questions #65-69   Date: _____
Questions #70-74   Date: _____
Questions #75-79   Date: _____
Questions #80-83   Date: _____
Questions #84-87   Date: _____

Scriptures

John 15:16   Date: _____
John 17:9–11   Date: _____
Romans 8:29–30   Date: _____
Proverbs 21:23   Date: _____
Proverbs 16:32   Date: _____
Proverbs 23:23   Date: _____
Psalm 27   Date: _____
Psalm 119:81–112   Date: _____

Bible Basics

The Books of the Bible   Date: _____

Hymns

Great is Thy Faithfulness Date: _____
Come Ye Sinners   Date: _____

AGE THIRTEEN
The Baptist Catechism

Questions #88-93   Date: _____
Questions #94-99   Date: _____
Questions #100-104   Date: _____
Questions #105-109   Date: _____
Questions #110-115   Date: _____

Scriptures

Philippians 2:5–13   Date: _____
Galatians 2:16   Date: _____
Ephesians 2:8–10   Date: _____
2 Corinthians 12:9   Date: _____
Isaiah 26:3–4   Date: _____
Proverbs 15:5   Date: _____
Psalm 119:113–136   Date: _____
Isaiah 55:6–11   Date: _____

Bible Basics

The Nicene Creed   Date: _____

Hymns

A Mighty Fortress is Our God Date: _____
Stand Up, Stand Up For Jesus Date: _____

Presented to:

_____

From:

_____

Date:

_____

TRUTH AND GRACE MEMORY BOOK

BOOK 2

Ages Ten to Thirteen

THOMAS K. ASCOL, EDITOR

©2017 Founders Press
P.O. Box 150931
Cape Coral, FL 33915
Phone (239) 772-1400
http://www.founders.org

ISBN: 978-1-943539-05-5

Unless otherwise indicated, all Scripture
quotations are from the ESV® Bible (The Holy
Bible, English Standard Version®), copyright ©
2001 by Crossway, a publishing ministry of Good
News Publishers. Used by permission. All rights
reserved.

Cover Design by Joshua Noom